INSIDE YOUR BODY

ALL ABOUT COLDS

FRANCESCA POTTS, RN

Consulting Editor, Diane Craig, MA/Reading Specialist

Super Sandcastle

An Imprint of Abdo Publishing
abdopublishing.com

ABDOPUBLISHING.COM

Published by Abdo Publishing, a division of ABDO, PO Box
398166, Minneapolis, Minnesota 55439. Copyright © 2018
by Abdo Consulting Group, Inc. International copyrights
reserved in all countries. No part of this book may be
reproduced in any form without written permission from
the publisher. Super SandCastle™ is a trademark and logo
of Abdo Publishing.

Printed in the United States of America,
North Mankato, Minnesota
062017
092017

Production: Mighty Media, Inc.
Editor: Liz Salzmann
Cover Photographs: Shutterstock
Interior Photographs: Mighty Media, Inc.; Shutterstock

Publisher's Cataloging-in-Publication Data
Names: Potts, Francesca, author.
Title: All about colds / by Francesca Potts, RN.
Description: Minneapolis, MN : Abdo Publishing, 2018. I Series:
    Inside your body
Identifiers: LCCN 2016962905 I ISBN 9781532111174 (lib. bdg.) I
    ISBN 9781680789027 (ebook)
Subjects: LCSH: Cold (Disease)--Juvenile literature. I Influenza--
    Juvenile literature. I Joints--Wounds and injuries--Juvenile
    literature.
Classification: DDC 616.2/05--dc23
LC record available at http://lccn.loc.gov/2016962905

Super SandCastle™ books are created by a team of professional
educators, reading specialists, and content developers around five
essential components—phonemic awareness, phonics, vocabulary,
text comprehension, and fluency—to assist young readers as they
develop reading skills and strategies and increase their general
knowledge. All books are written, reviewed, and leveled for guided
reading, early reading intervention, and Accelerated Reader™
programs for use in shared, guided, and independent reading
and writing activities to support a balanced approach to literacy
instruction.

CONTENTS

YOUR BODY

AREAS MOST AFFECTED BY A COLD

You're amazing! So is your body.

Most of the time your body works just fine. It lets you go to school, play with friends, and more. But sometimes you feel sick or part of you hurts.

One sickness your body can get is a cold. Most people get a cold at least once a year. For this reason, it is also called the *common cold*.

RHINOVIRUS (rye-noh-VYE-ruhs)

a tiny organism that causes colds

ALL ABOUT
COLDS

A cold is caused by a **virus**. The virus can be in the air you breathe. It can also be on something you touch. That is how it gets in your body. Then the virus grows inside cells such as blood cells.

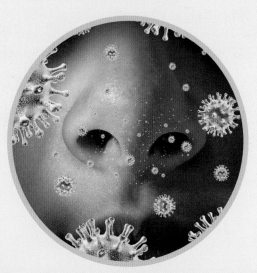

COLD VIRUS

DROP OF
BLOOD

WHITE
BLOOD
CELL

Your **immune system** detects **viruses**. The white blood cells in your blood are the first to react. They work with the rest of your immune system to kill the virus! This fight is what causes cold **symptoms**. When the battle is over, the virus is gone and you feel better.

COLD, HARD
FACTS

Kids just like you can get up to ten colds each year. But each time, your **immune system** improves. It learns better ways to fight the **virus**. This means you'll get fewer colds as you get older.

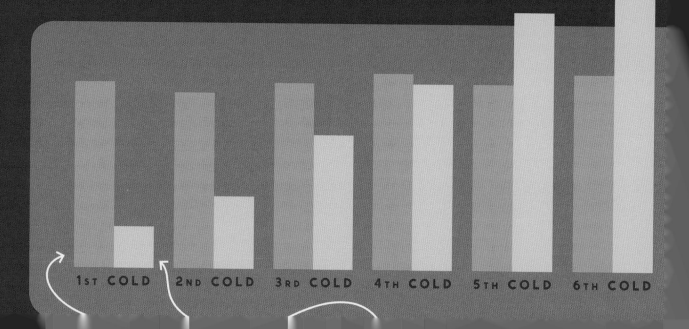

1ST COLD   2ND COLD   3RD COLD   4TH COLD   5TH COLD   6TH COLD

Cold Season

Most colds occur between August and April. Why? It has to do with the school year. In school, kids spend more time near others who may have colds. This increases their chances of catching a cold.

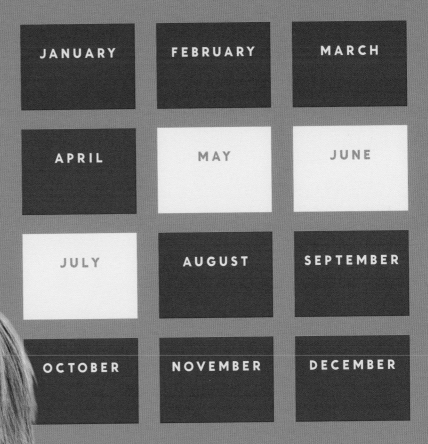

JANUARY	FEBRUARY	MARCH
APRIL	MAY	JUNE
JULY	AUGUST	SEPTEMBER
OCTOBER	NOVEMBER	DECEMBER

Sick Days

A cold is the top illness that keeps kids home from school. It is also the top reason kids go to the doctor.

CATCHING
COLDS

There are many ways you can catch a cold. Cold **germs** can travel through the air. Imagine someone near you has a cold. When he breathes out, his germs get into the air. When you breathe in, you may take in those germs.

You can also catch a cold from direct contact. A person with a cold may cough into her hands. Or, she may not wash her hands after blowing her nose. If you touch her hands, you can pick up her cold **germs**.

SIGNS
AND SYMPTOMS

HOW DO YOU KNOW THAT YOU HAVE A COLD?
HERE ARE SOME SYMPTOMS.

**RUNNY NOSE,
SNIFFLING, AND
SNEEZING**

SORE THROAT

COUGHING

**MUSCLE ACHES
AND HEADACHE**

LOW FEVER

**MUCUS BECOMES
THICK AND TURNS
YELLOW OR GREEN**

Every cold doesn't necessarily cause all of these **symptoms**. You might feel some but not others. Cold symptoms start about two to three days after getting a **virus**. The symptoms usually last about seven to ten days.

Cold Timeline

DAY	DAY	DAY	DAY	DAY	DAY	DAY	DAY	DAY	DAY	DAY	DAY	DAY
1	2	3	4	5	6	7	8	9	10	11	12	13

■ VIRUS ENTERS BODY   ■ SYMPTOMS START   ■ SYMPTOMS CONTINUE

COLD OR FLU?

The flu is another common illness caused by **viruses**. Flu **symptoms** can be similar to cold symptoms. Here are how these illnesses are different.

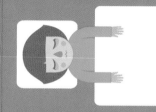

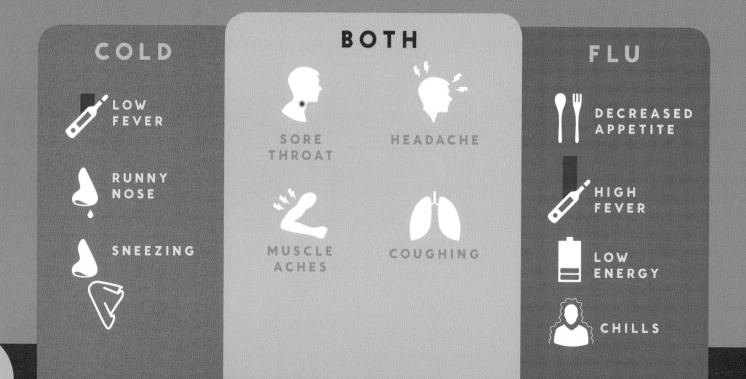

COLD

- LOW FEVER
- RUNNY NOSE
- SNEEZING

BOTH

- SORE THROAT
- HEADACHE
- MUSCLE ACHES
- COUGHING

FLU

- DECREASED APPETITE
- HIGH FEVER
- LOW ENERGY
- CHILLS

Prevention

One big difference between a cold and flu is prevention. There is a vaccination that helps prevent the flu **virus**. But there is not one for the cold virus.

{ FAST FACT }

A strong cough can push air out at nearly 500 miles per hour (800 kmh)!

IMMUNE ARMY

Cold **symptoms** are no fun. But they are signs that your body is fighting the cold! Your **immune system** creates **mucus** when it fights a cold. This causes you to get a runny nose.

WHITE BLOOD CELL

Cough

Sometimes you breathe in **mucus** when you have a cold. This causes coughing.

Fever

Your **immune system** may also cause a fever. This is harmful to the **virus**. The virus cannot survive at higher temperatures. So, it begins to die off.

MANAGING
SYMPTOMS

Although your **immune system** fights a cold, there are things you can do to help it!

Treatment

Medicine cannot cure a cold. But medicines and other remedies can help manage **symptoms**. An adult can help you choose the best **treatment** for your cold.

Rest

Avoid activities that use a lot of energy. Then your body will have more energy to fight the cold.

Stay Hydrated

Drink extra water. This helps keep your **mucus** thin. Then it's easier to cough it up or blow it out your nose.

TREATMENTS

There are many medicines and natural remedies for cold **symptoms**. Ask an adult which **treatments** you should try.

MEDICINES

COUGH EXPECTORANT
Helps the body cough up **mucus**

NASAL DECONGESTANT
Unclogs a stuffed nose

PAIN RELIEVER
Relieves fever and sore throat pain

THROAT LOZENGES AND SPRAYS
Relieve sore throat pain

NATURAL REMEDIES

SALT WATER
Gargling with salt water soothes a sore throat

WARM LIQUID
Helps mucus flow from your body and soothes a sore throat

ZINC SUPPLEMENTS AND VITAMIN C
Strengthen your **immune system**

WHEN TO SEE
A DOCTOR

Most of the time, medicines and natural remedies provide cold relief. But sometimes you may need to see a doctor. Tell an adult if you develop these **symptoms**.

- Coughing up a lot of thick **mucus**

- Shortness of breath or **wheezing**

- Feeling very tired for many days

- Not wanting to eat or drink

- Increasing headache or throat pain

- Problems swallowing

- Fever above 101 **degrees** Fahrenheit (38°C) lasting more than one day

- Fever above 103 degrees Fahrenheit (39°C)

- Chest pain

- Earache

PREVENTION

Colds are a common sickness. And there are many **treatments** for **symptoms**. But the very best way to fight colds is to prevent them. Follow these tips to stay healthy!

WASH YOUR HANDS OFTEN.

AVOID SHARING FORKS AND SPOONS WITH OTHERS.

ALWAYS COVER YOUR COUGHS AND SNEEZES.

CLEAN TOYS AND PLAY AREAS WELL AND OFTEN.

GET PLENTY OF SLEEP.

DRINK A LOT OF WATER.

EXERCISE.

DEGREE - the unit used to measure temperature.

GARGLE - to hold a liquid in the throat and make it bubble with air from the lungs.

GERM - a tiny, living organism that can make people sick.

IMMUNE SYSTEM - the system of the body that fights infection and disease.

MUCUS - a slippery, sticky substance produced by the body.

SYMPTOM - a noticeable change in the normal working of the body.

TREATMENT - medical or surgical care for a sickness or an injury.

VIRUS - any of a group of tiny organisms that cause diseases. They grow and multiply in living cells.

WHEEZE - to breathe with difficulty and often with a whistling sound.

GLOSSARY